# Transplanted
## How Immigrating
## Changed our Lives

The English Learners of Carthage
High School

Edited by Zach Spiering

To our families who got us this far

# CONTENTS

# FORWARD

Dear Reader,

You had the opportunity to choose from a nearly infinite selection of books, but you chose this brief tome. Thank you for taking a chance on a group of authors you have probably never heard of.

I cannot promise that in the following pages, you will find the most riveting prose in the English language. You will not likely read here the most skilled poetry. The essays are unlikely to be the most compelling you will ever read.

I can promise that in the following pages you will find truth.

These are the words of immigrant teenagers who have, for various reasons and in various ways, come from Latin America to, of all places, a small town in Missouri. Each has their own story, their own motivations, their own voice. Yet collectively, they give us a glimpse at a world that is surprising in both its familiarity and its novelty.

I ask, that as you read these pages, you will put your politics aside and allow your feelings about immigration policy to take a back seat. I do not say this because these issues are unimportant. Nor do I assume a particular stance. The issues are far more complex than most people give them credit for, regardless of what side they end up on.

I ask only that you would approach these stories with a different purpose, namely to appreciate the humanity in people who are often seen only in statistics and soundbites. Take off your shoes and slip into the sneakers of a group of kids that came from a little different neighborhood than you did.

Sometimes when I share an anecdote about one of my students, someone will inevitably ask: is that typical? Do they all do this? Or someone might ask the equally impossible question: what do the Hispanics think of this new immigration policy?

What is typical? Is my experience typical of all white people who grew up in the Midwest? Can I speak for what white Midwesterners think of any topic. Get any three of us in a room and you will likely get four opinions about your issue. My students are no less individuals, not a block of similarity but a diversity of characters: scholars and slackers, athletes and couch potatoes, devout and heretics, socialites and loners.

I have had the opportunity to teach this incredible group of students whose worlds, as you will read, are defined by river crossings and detention centers but equally by pop music and soccer tryouts. These are kids who daily face adversity and must determine to overcome it. Along the way, they have given a voice to so many who share their journey. We are a nation of immigrants, and the stories contained in these pages add another layer to our story, the story of America.

Zach Spiering

# NATIVE SOIL

## GUATEMALA BEACH
Anonymous

Salt water in eyes
Waves are big and knock you out
They pull your shorts down


## BROKEN
Santiago Chavez Garcia

This is how my arm broke. First, we were preparing everything to celebrate the quinceanera of my cousin. We started decorating the house. We put up balloons and other decorations. After that we went to the store for the ingredients for the tamales we were going to make, and then we went back home to prepare the food. Finally, the time came that we were going to celebrate the birthday of my cousin. She told me that she was nervous about her quinceanera. I reminded her that she wanted to celebrate it.

She told me that she knew that but she was still nervous.

After that I asked my other cousins if we could play tag; they said yes and then we started to play. We were all fine until one of them shoved me. Suddenly, I was flying over a car. When I landed down the road, one of my cousins helped me to get up. The others went to tell my family because I was crying about the pain.

My grandmother was very worried about what had happened to me, she asked what happened and one of my cousins told her that we were playing and they pushed me and a car hit me.

Later my grandmother called my mother, who is here in the USA, asking to send money to take me to the hospital. So my mother asked my grandmother how I broke my arm and my grandmother explained to her. Then she was a little angry at me.

After that, they took me to the hospital and put the cast on me. The doctor said to me I need to be careful with my arm.

## EDUCATION
### Anonymous

Education in Guatemala is okay, but not too good like here. When I was in Guatemala, the school I used to go to was not enough for me because they had a lot of students and they did not teach what they are supposed to teach you. You don't learn much like that.

One day my mom asked me, "Do you wanna have a better future?"

I said, "yeah!"

And then she asked, "Do you want to go to the U.S.A.?

I said I did but I asked her what about her and my sisters. She said, "Don't worry about us. I just want a better future for you. I don't want you to be like the other kids who sell drugs and steal."

When I first went to school in the US, I was so lost and I was about to start crying but I reminded myself that this is what I want and I have it now.

Now every time that I talk with my mom she always reminds me when I first went to school in Guatemala. But, yeah, everything here is different than in Guatemala.

# UPROOTED

## TO HAVE A BETTER LIFE
Freddy Guinac

At the beginning of my life, I was in Guatemala. My parents left me with my grandparents when I was one year old. Sometimes I missed school in Guatemala because I was working with my grandfather at the farm. I had to wake up at 4 a.m. to help my grandfather to bring water to the farm to feed the cows, chickens, pigs, and ducks. The most important thing was when we worked in the field.

I started working at the farm when I was ten years old. At first, I didn't like it because it was so hot and boring. When I turned eleven I began to like it more, but still not much because there are scorpions and I am scared of them. I remember I was in the cornfield when a scorpion stung me and I started crying in the field. My grandfather asked what happened, and I said there was a scorpion in the cornfield. I went back home because I didn't feel good at the time.

By the time I turned thirteen I liked the work because my grandparents sometimes gave me money for working in the field. We worked from 7 A.M to 12 P.M and we went back to work at 2 P.M to 6 P.M. We got tired. We worked in the field too much every week.

I was about to turn fourteen when my mom and dad called me to say, "Son, do you want to live with us in the U.S.A?" I was so happy to go to the U.S.A, but at the same time, I was sad because I didn't want to leave my grandparents alone. My dad said, ' Son you have to decide if you want to come here or if you want to stay in Guatemala.

I finally said to my dad, "I am going to live with you dad,"

I celebrated Christmas with my grandparents and then the next day my parents had me come to the U.S.A. I was so sad that day. I still remember seeing my grandparents for the last time. I was crying on the bus and the next day I was so sad I didn't talk or eat.

I was in Mexico for one week. When I was passing through Mexico I visited some places where it was so horrible because there were people with weapons. Some places were cool and others were hot.

I was on the bus when a person started screaming on the bus I didn't know why. Then the driver stopped the bus and then he called the police to take the person from the bus because he was screaming at the people on the bus. The police came and I heard the police say "Come out. We want to talk with you. If you don't, you're going to jail."

He said, "take me to jail," and the police took the person to jail. It was so funny because he went to jail.

I came to the border with Mexico and the United States. I crossed the river that was near the United States. Then the Immigration officer came and he said, "Hey guys, come with me."

The officer took me to jail. Then I saw a lot of guys in the jail. I was in jail for about seven hours then they called me to take me to the Detention Center.

When I got to the Detention Center I thought, this looked so cool. It was a good place to stay but at the same time, it wasn't because we had to follow rules. We had to sleep at 6 p.m. in the afternoon and then we had to wake up at 7 a.m. People had to wait for months or years to get out of the Detention Center. But I never waited months in that place, only one week. Then they called me to the office of the detention center and said, "Fredy Guinac you are going with your parents today, everything is paid. The only thing you have to do is to put all your stuff in your suitcase then you are free to go. Congratulations, Fredy and have a good trip."

I said "Thanks."

When I went on the airplane everything wasn't so beautiful. I waited for the airplane for 2 hours, until I heard it said to stand in line and get my ticket ready.

When I exited the airplane, I saw my parents for the first time. I cried a lot because it was the first time I saw my parents in a long time. I still remember my mom saying," Welcome, son, to the United States. Now you are going to have a better life."

I cried again and I hugged my mom and my dad too, and then we went home. My mom gave me food and bought clothes and everything. One week later when I was living with my parents my mom put me in school to study and learn English. I went to junior high for the first time.

My first day was so great because I made new friends and two months later I had a girlfriend. At the junior high every day I was so happy to go back to school again to see my girlfriend and talk to her. She only spoke a little Spanish. I taught her to speak Spanish and she taught me to speak English just a little bit. The most important thing is she loved me and she didn't care if I could speak English.

After six months living here, Immigration sent me a permit to live legally in the United States. I found a job working at a restaurant. They didn't pay very well but it's okay because I liked the job. It was kind of easy. I started to make money at fifteen years old and I saved all my money and three months later bought a car. At fifteen years old, I bought it by myself. I always wanted to have my car. I knew this was my life but my dad warned me that if I bought the car it was going to have a lot of problems. But two weeks later he said the car is so cool to drive he asked "Can I use it for one week?"

I said "Sure dad." He loved my car

My life was so different when I bought my car because I never thought that I was going to have a car when I was fifteen years old. I told my parents. "I never thought that I was going to have a better life, I have a better life because of you, Mom and Dad", I said to my parents. "Thanks, Dad and Mom for giving me a better life, but also, "Thanks to God, too. I have a better life. Thanks, God!"

## AMERICAN KID
### Christian Juarez Chavez

There once was a kid who lived in Guatemala but he was about to move to a different country. I did not know anything about it when my family told me that they were planning to move to the USA to be with family and friends that we have not seen for a long time. About two weeks later, they told me that I will be the first one to go and I will live with some family members and stay there for a while. I moved from Guatemala in November.

It all started when I left Guatemala. I had to ride a car for an hour and then I got to the bus station. Once the bus reached its destination I had to get on a different bus. Sometimes I rode a bus more than a day. I had to sleep in the seat of the bus. It was uncomfortable but I got used to it because I got on different buses. One thing that I did not like from buses is that they are very slow. One thing that I like about this trip is that I visited different places in Mexico. I had never visited Mexico so this was my first time. I ate tacos. I do not remember the name of the other food that I ate but it tasted excellent. It had rice, avocado, and beef. I ate different types of food and some of them tasted terrible.

After four days I got in Laredo TX and got on the last bus. I rode the bus from Texas to Missouri. Once I got in Missouri my family who lived in the USA came and picked me up from the bus station. After one week I went to school. The name of the school is CIC. I met my teacher and then I met different people. After two months passed my family came and I moved and lived with them in a house.

I would like people to visit Mexico. It is a good place to visit.

## MEETING MY PARENTS
### Melfor Lopez

My parents live here in the United States so that is the main reason why I came here. I missed them all the time and I decided to come and see them. My father came to the United States for the first time when I was two years old, and my mother, when I was five. So, I came to this country to meet my parents and to have a better life in this country.

My trip began in Guatemala. Early in the morning I left at 7:30 a.m. from my house. The person who brought me was a 40-year-old man. He took us in his car to a place in Guatemala called Tecun Uman, it was ten hours by car until we reached the hotel.

I traveled by car and sometimes I rode the bus during my trip to the United States. I stopped in Mexico and I traveled only by bus. The police always stopped the bus during my trip, to check if an immigrant was on the bus. When the review was over, the man who brought me had his contacts to let us pass without a problem.

In Mexico I stayed for twenty-seven days in a place

called Tampico. There I slept in a hotel called "Maria Reyes". In the hotel there were restaurants. The man who brought me told me that anytime when I was hungry I could go down to order some food, because I had already paid for everything in the hotel. I didn't like the food they made, because it was Mexican food and is really different from the food of my country. The food I liked the most was roast beef, chicken mole, and fried eggs.

I left that hotel on a Wednesday because they were going to take me to the United States. I was going to try to cross the river at a town called Rio Bravo. I did not want to cross from there because there were many police in that place and they could take me. I returned to a house where I was passing the days to take some rest and take a shower because it was already night and I was going to try to cross again during the next morning. I crossed the river on a jet ski. It was very fast and fun, I got to McAllen, Texas. I stayed five days and then I was taken to Houston, Texas, where my family was going to meet me, finally.

When they took me to Houston Texas, I was very happy because I was going to see my parents, but at the same time I was really nervous. When I finally looked at my parents and relatives I got tears of happiness, I was really happy to finally see all of them again, and it is a day I will never forget.

# EVERYTHING WE LEFT BEHIND
## Christian Juarez Chavez

What do immigrants leave behind? When immigrants have to migrate, they have to think twice and it's a very complicated decision. Immigrants have to leave their homes and cities where they grew up. They also have to leave family members.

You also have to leave behind your language when you immigrate. My own experience of learning another language is that it takes a lot of time and is not that easy. Learning a new language is a privilege that not everyone has but if you're going to learn another language, things might get confusing for you. You have to learn the new grammar and vocabulary and other different rules that this language has. According to "How Learning Happens" a recent study out of Philadelphia tracked kindergarteners who were learning English, it took four years for students to master the language.

How hard is English for those that only speak Spanish at home? "How Learning Happens" states that "students whose home language was Spanish were less likely to reach 'considerably proficient' than other groups." This study also mentions an eleven-year-old immigrant that came to the USA and he said that there haven't been big changes since he moved. Everywhere he goes, he always speaks Spanish. Speaking your home language, though, can make it hard for you to learn another language.

Most immigrants had to leave their home country for more opportunities such as education that their home country didn't have, but this journey can be very dangerous. According to Amnesty International, some people risk falling prey to human trafficking and other form of exploitation. UN News states that "Since 2014, more than 3,800 (migrant) deaths have been recorded across the continent. More deaths have occurred along the border between the United States and Mexico. Many immigrants have lost their lives along the Rio Bravo/Rio Grande which runs between Texas and Mexico.

In conclusion, it's a hard decision for immigrants to move to America because we have to leave so many things.

## IN THE MIDDLE OF THE SOCCER GAME
Anonymous

One day I was playing soccer like normal because that was the only way that we could entertain ourselves, when I heard my mom yell my name and my brother's name. Both of us left the game and came running to her. She sent us to the room where we stayed. I thought she was going to hit us or something but I didn't remember doing anything wrong. Then she came into the room, and my grandparents were there too. She told us with tears in her eyes that we were going to the North. In Guatemala we say " Nos vamos a ir para Norte" which basically means we are going to the U.S.A.

The only thing I did was hang my head and cry because we didn't have plans to move to the U.S.A. My brother that was beside me started crying because he knew that it was going to be hard leaving my family. It was especially hard for me to leave my grandpa because he was the person that taught me everything from casting a net to knowing how to swim. He was the person who taught me how to wield a machete. We would do everything together. We would go fishing together and he gave me advice every time that I didn't feel well. Then I remember asking my mom when we were living. She said in two days.

The next day I had to solve a problem. That problem was telling my girlfriend that I was leaving Guatemala to go to the United States. Then she started crying because she didn't want me to leave. I told her not to make it harder. I told her to be happy with someone else, but she said that she wouldn't be happy with anyone but me. The only thing I did was give her a goodbye kiss, because I didn't know when I was coming back. I knew that It was going to be for a while. So, I left her and the only thing that passed through my mind was not to look back or I would make a decision that I was going to regret in the future. I left her house running.

When I got home and I only had a couple hours left before bedtime, so I started packing my stuff that I was going to take. The next morning, I woke up sad because I didn't want to leave my family. But I didn't have any other choice but to go.

So, I left home around 12:00 p.m. Me and my brother and mom were coming together. After leaving the house I remember that we had to take a trip of three hours, probably four. After that long ride we got to a gas station where we had to wait for a bus to take us to Reinosa, Mexico. I don't know how long it took to get there but it felt so long. While riding on the bus I remember that migration took my mom out of the bus for questioning. It didn't take too long to get her back on the bus.

Then we got to Reinosa. We stayed there for two days. The man that was guiding us said that some people were going to pick us up in a Tahoe vehicle. The two days passed and then the Tahoe came. We rode the Tahoe where the driver would take us near the Rio Bravo (Rio Grande). While riding the Tahoe we had to lay down so people around wouldn't see us. The Tahoe arrived at the river and told us to get down fast. We got down as fast as we could and he said to wait here and not to move. Then a vehicle came full of other people that were crossing the river with us. It was followed by another vehicle that was full of people, people that were going to help us cross the river. They were called only by their nicknames, not their actual names. They were tall dudes, they looked really young, probably eighteen or nineteen years old.

After crossing the river, one of the guys told us to choose our way. At the distance we saw a water tower then we walked to the water tower. It took us 15 minutes to get there. While walking I fell down and got mud all over my face. We got to the water tower and sat down there and we heard a four-wheeler coming toward us. And it was a border patrol agent. The patrol agent told us all that were relatives to stay together, or mothers with children.

After all that happened a patrol van came and took us under a bridge. The agent told us to take off our belts, our laces from our shoes and jewelry. Then he took us to a cell where they treat you like a prisoner. The cells stank of urine. And the food that they gave there was horrible. The type of food that they gave there was a sandwich with ham and cheese and a fruit and a juice. But the sandwich smelled so bad that it made you throw up. My brother and mom just drank the juice but didn't eat the sandwiches.

At the time we went to sleep we didn't know at what time it was because there were no clocks and no windows. The only thing we knew was when the officers turned off the lights. While sleeping at night there were people crying so we couldn't sleep because of people crying, asking to be taken out of there, that they just didn't want to be there. Some people had been there for months, others, a week or two.

On the second day I just didn't want to stay there anymore and started crying. After the two and a half days passed, a lady came into the door and started calling our names. She didn't tell us where we were going. Then a patrol van was waiting for us outside. We rode the van and I thought we were going to be sent back to our country but no instead we got put in another jail. There, at least, they gave us better food and a couch and a blanket that looked like aluminum to cover us. The next day, I remember asking an officer what day it was. He told me "Es Miercoles" Which means it's Wednesday. And the officer was so nice that he brought a soccer ball for us to play inside the jail.

Thursday afternoon we were taken to a shelter where it was full of nuns and pastors. When we got there the nuns were lined up, clapping for us, meaning that we made it safe here we are going to bring you cloth and food. Once we got inside the shelter the nuns offered us clothes, shoes, and food. I remember the first meal we ate - chicken soup. After that they took us where we were going to take a shower. We hadn't had a shower in four days. Before showering they asked our sizes for shirts, pants and shoes. While showering they brought us our clothes.

We spend the night there. Friday passed and Saturday came at night around 9:00 P.M. and the officer checked if our tickets were already paid and yes, they were already paid. At 10:00 P.M. Saturday night we boarded a bus that was going to take us to Dallas, Texas. We got to Dallas and had to wait there for three more hours, and we ate nothing at all that night. Then a man approached us and asked if we had eaten and my mom told him we hadn't. Then the man offered to buy some sandwiches for the three of us. And he just said not to move from where we were. He actually got the sandwiches for us and chips and some sodas.

We finally had some food in our stomachs. Then, after waiting in the bus station for three hours we finally got to board a bus again, a bus that was going to take us to our destination. I don't remember how long it was going to take but I guess it was going to take about fifteen hours because of all the stops that the bus driver took. I remember falling asleep in the bus.

Our destination was Indianapolis, Indiana, where our uncle and his wife were supposed to be waiting for us inside the bus station. When we pulled up to the station, I decided to go ask the bus driver if this was our stop. He said, "Yes we're here," and then my mom saw my uncle outside the bus. I remember getting there at night around 8 P.M. Sunday evening. I was happy but at the same time sad because I hadn't talked to my family in Guatemala since we left. At the time, the only thing I wanted to do was sleep and wake up fresh.

I knew that the United States was a country with a better future. That's why we came here for a better life and better future.

# TAKING ROOT

## DEAR AMERICA: WHAT YOU NEED TO KNOW ABOUT THE IMMIGRANTS WHO LIVE HERE
Mariana Lugo Perez

We didn't come here to steal your jobs and money, we don't talk bad about you when we speak in our native language, and the fact that we celebrate our own culture does not mean we don't respect yours.

What you have to know about immigrants who live here is that they sacrifice a big part of their culture and language. Part of that is because most of the people around them do not speak the same language, and the other reason is that sometimes the people that don't speak the language prefer them to speak English, because they do not understand.

People seem to think we are talking about them when we talk in our native language, because they don't understand. They probably believe that it will be really easy for us to make fun of them in their faces and they will have no idea what we are talking about. But most of the immigrants are good people that prefer to respect people, so they don't do this type of behavior.

According to The UN Migration Agency, "All people – without discrimination – possess rights and fundamental freedoms and that States have a prime responsibility and duty to respect, protect and fulfil those rights and freedoms." This is in contrast to those people that get angry when someone talks in another language.

Most of the time, we are aware of the fact that English is not the only spoken language in The United States, but in my daily life I hear comments like: "We are in America, speak English" or "Why are you speaking Spanish?" That should not be a reason for them to make us feel bad about our ethnicity or culture. Most of the time immigrants could speak more than two languages and could make some people jealous for the knowledge those people have. They would take it as disrespect. But for the people that don't speak English they could get even more angry and find it very disrespectful.

An example of this would be my parents. My sister and I have a good level of English but our parents don't speak or understand anything in English. I find it really disrespectful that some people say that immigrants that do not speak English are lazy, because I know how hard my parents work to give me a living and food on the table. Because of that they don't have the time to study the language.

Because I know all of this from my own experience, I can tell you that what you need to know about the immigrants that live here in the U.S is not necessarily all their culture, or to speak the same language as them. A better option is just to know how to respect different cultures and people. We sacrifice a lot of ourselves and we have the right to share our culture with other countries, but especially we have the right to be free of discrimination. Then we all will be ready to expand the knowledge of culture, language, or race. In conclusion, everyone can decide to be part of the movement and not part of the problem.

LIVING IN THIS TOWN
Melfor Lopez Ramos

What it feels like living in this town,
I'm close to everyone I love,
everything I've ever dreamed of.
It gives me a new beginning
a fresh new start
I reflect on myself as a lion,
looking for new adventures.
Soccer is my passion
rolling new opportunities.
From my faraway land weather is plain,
Unlike my hometown, in Carthage
boring no longer exists.

NORMA
Mariana Lugo Perez

One person that helped me was Norma, the secretary of my last high school. When I first came here to the United States I didn't know anything about culture, idioms, customs, etc. Norma helped my sister and me with English. Thanks to her I know this level of English and she helped me to not be so shy, because yes, in the past I was shyer than now. Norma was the person that helped me most in all my three years in the United States.

## CLASS RULES
### Santiago Chavez Garcia

Put away your phone
Pay attention when the class
starts. Sit in your chair!


## ON IMMIGRATING
### Anonymous

Immigrating to the United States has more positive aspects than negative aspects for you and you and it will also bring positive and negative aspects to your family.

Learning English allows you to communicate in a foreign language. It gave me the ability to get to know more people and to communicate with them. Getting a new career in the United States is a smart decision because it will benefit you and your family and your economic status and your future. You may also broaden your experience by taking on a new job or learning new skills.

Immigrating to the United States of America helps you with your documents for your citizenship. According to usa.gov, citizens get to go in and outside the country. For you to have a residency or being a citizen helps you and assists you from being deported. Having a residency or being a citizen also helps your children to be a citizen and they get to be born here.

Immigrating to America could also cause some consequences for you and your friends, especially to your family. It was hard for me leaving my home country, my friends, and especially my family. You might feel weird being in a foreign country, especially if you do not have family or someone you know. It will be hard to find somewhere to live and somewhere to work. Fortunately, I had my parents here and some other family. It will be hard to speak the local language. You would also miss the time you spent with your family or friends in your home country. You will miss your country as well.

In conclusion, immigrating to the United States brings good benefits and also some consequences, but I think that immigrating to the United States is generally more good than bad.

## IF YOU ARE GOING TO DISNEYLAND, DON'T FORGET TO CHECK THE WEATHER FIRST.
### Mariana Lugo Perez

On December 12, my family shared with my sister and me that we were going to Disneyland. I didn't believe it at first. We were really happy and excited. We prepared to travel to California to spend our first Christmas with my uncle after a long time apart from him. I didn't know if I was happier about seeing my uncle again, or for the fact that I was going to Disneyland. We met a lot of families, especially Brenda's family, she is the daughter of my grandma's sister. She worked in Disneyland. She gave the tickets to my sister and me, for free. I was thankful to her. She is an amazing person.

It was a shiny and cold morning in Anaheim, California. My family and I woke up early that day, we drove to the house of my grandma's sister, and we ate breakfast there, prepared our backpacks, and chatted with the family. The weather started to get really hot, like any other day in Anaheim. Brenda drove to Disneyland's entrance, and the moment we entered Disney, the weather started to change. The sky started to get dark from all the clouds, and the air got cold. We didn't mind at all, we were enjoying the firsts attractions, at the right side of Disneyland. We walked and ate a lot. I remember that we ate bread that they made there; it was like French bread with butter, but actually tasted a little bit more like cheese and onion with species. It reminds me of the butter that my grandma made with the milk of cows. And we ate pretzels, which I didn't like. They were very salty, and I almost threw up. We also ate a really sweet ice cream of chocolate and vanilla that was so flavorful and delicious. We walked a lot, we didn't stop, not even a minute; at that moment, I could barely feel my feet on the ground.

We stopped at the theater show of "Frozen", the "attraction" where we spent the most time, about an hour. During the line we ate the sandwiches that my grandma made for us, toasted cheese and a little bit of spicy taste. That is the moment when the weather changed completely, but now we were there, just waiting in line so we couldn't move. The rain started, it got cold and foggy.

Getting tired, bored, and at that time, really wet from the rain, we got into the theater and we watched the show. The play was about an hour-long and was funny and kind of sad too. The actors of the play look really like the real versions of the animated movie. In the end, when we got out of the theater, it was not raining anymore. Enjoying the attractions and atmosphere of that cold rainy but occasionally sunny day. At the other attractions, we didn't spend time in line, and at the moment started to rain again, we were in a line with big umbrellas that protected us. The funny thing is that the line's attraction was "Nemo", and at the end, we got a little bit wet again.

Because of the rain, we were not able to watch the fireworks. My sister and I felt sad. But the good thing is that my uncle lived close to Disneyland, and the other nights that we spent in Anaheim, we saw the fireworks at the balcony of my uncle's house.

We thought we were prepared for everything, but we forgot to check the weather that day. Now, my family can't go out of the house if we don't look first at the weather for that day.

## THE MUSIC THAT MOVES ME
Anonymous

Trap is the type of music that moves me. The artist that I like to listen to is XXXTentacion. Trap uses a lot of instruments such as the drum machine. It's a nice instrument but it is hard to play. It takes a lot of practice to do it perfectly. The best part about trap is that you can listen to it in English and in Spanish. I like to listen to it in both languages. I think everyone has listened to XXXTentacion. He was so famous until he passed away.

## SOCCER GAME
The W4 Class

Gloves girded by the goaltender
Shinguard, shoes and jersey
Benchwarmers drink water
While the striker takes his first penalty.

## BRAVELY WOMEN
### Mariana Lugo Perez

Woman fighting bravely
Woman fighting bravely, angrily
Fighting bravely, angrily, loudly
Bravely, angrily, loudly, necessarily
Even when others are complaining.

Delicate as a flower
Growing by my own shine
Hiding behind the undercover
I'm stronger than I know

Hidden to myself
Keeping quiet, my rough self
I keep my soul inside a shelf
I just want to be myself.

.

# AN UNEXPECTED PRUNING

## QUARANTINE
Anonymous

The first day when I heard that everyone was getting quarantined I thought that everyone was just playing, and then I watched the news and all the hospitals were full.

When the COVID started, I was in Los Angeles. We went for vacation, but when we were in Los Angeles, they told us that we couldn't go out. We were in L.A for just one week and then we came back to Missouri. Everyone in Los Angeles was in quarantine, and when we came back to Carthage, everyone was in their homes. There was no one in the street or in the stores, but the quarantine was so difficult and that's all I have to say about the quarantine.

Then after two weeks a member of my family got COVID-19. He had gotten arrested, and when he went to jail, he got infected with COVID there in jail After one week, he died.

After one family member died, six weeks later another one of my family got COVID, and he went to the hospital. He got a positive test and they told him to go home to quarantine for two weeks. He is good now. But right now (at the time of writing) one of my cousins is in quarantine because he was close to some friends and he got COVID. The principal told him that he had to be in quarantine for two weeks. Now he's back to school.

2020 was one of the hardest years in history with COVID 19. It was one of sicknesses and epidemics. It seemed that almost everyone in the world got sick with COVID 19 and a lot of people died because of that. Right now, COVID 19 is still killing a lot of people in the world and no one knows the cure for the epidemic. Many of the scientists are working to find the cure.

## MY WORRIES DURING QUARANTINE.
### Freddy Guinac

During the spring break last year, I spent a lot of time playing video games on my phone, but I was working at that time. Me and my friend went out to play sports or at the gym to do exercise. It was a bad day when my family and I were in quarantine, where my mom works.

A woman transmitted the virus to us. The person who passed the virus to us was contagious with COVID-19. Jasper Country gave us 12 days of quarantine. At that time, I was working but I stopped working because of the quarantine.

After we finished the quarantine, we had a party to celebrate. It was over for my family. After that my life situation was so different because I didn't trust other people when they came close to me. I have to wear a facemask at the stores and other places. I don't like to use face masks because I can't breathe well.

I was watching TV at my home and I got nervous about dying during the pandemic. I told my Mom "this year it's different from the others". We are six feet away from other people.

Every day that passed, I was so sad thinking about how life is going to be in the future, with this pandemic. I wondered if it was going to be normal again if doctors found a medicine or cure for this virus. I missed the days when I went out with my friends to buy food and visit places. I missed school because I missed seeing my friends, talking with girls and seeing my teachers.

I was waiting for August to go back to school to see my friends. Now I'm here at school, but I'm going to miss school because I am a senior and it's almost my graduation.

## DAY AT THE LAKE
Mariana Lugo Perez

Spending time with my family at home, is how my quarantine story begins, at the last week of quarantine. During all the quarantine my family and I didn't go anywhere. We really followed along quarantine guidelines. But the last week, my family and I went on a trip to Springfield. We went to a lake in Springfield. I actually do not know the name of that lake, but I can say that it was really pretty, and the water of the lake was cold because the lake has a lot of trees around. There was a lot of families spending time together.

Even though the water looks really green, the people there were swimming. They all were swimming and trying to forget about the virus around us. They all looked really happy. It was a really weird experience seeing all those people with their masks on when they were in the lake with their families.

After that my family and I went to eat a picnic. We ate sandwiches and chips, and drank soda. There was a family with two really big and scary dogs that came up to us trying to eat our food. It was really scary, but the dogs turned out to actually be really cute and friendly. They didn't want to eat our food, they wanted to play with us. We laughed because it was funny how all of us were scared of them.

After we finished our picnic we decided to go check out some universities and colleges that we might attend when my sister and I finish high school. We went to only two of them, because it was getting late and my dad had to turn back home to take care of the goats and cows that he just bought the week before. We went back home, and we watched a movie together.

My final thoughts about this, is that people try to keep going with their lives, even if we all have a difficult time. I will try to keep going with my daily life even with this pandemic around.

# ACKNOWLEDGEMENTS

We would like to acknowledge Matt Huntley and the leadership at Carthage R9 Schools for allowing us to complete this project, Lancelot Schaubert for his guidance, F.C. Shultz for helping us format and publish this book, Emeli Jimenez for editing and comments, and finally, we want to thank Mark Neuenschwander and the Joplin Toad for helping us make this a reality.

Transplanted

# ABOUT THE AUTHORS

This book is written by English learners, immigrant teens who made their home in Carthage Missouri. They are collectively: honest, brilliant, ornery, loud, thoughtful, shy, sneaky, rash, annoying, hilarious, and blunt. Some of them wish to remain anonymous.

The editorial team consists of Mr. Spiering's advanced English learners' class. If you find any errors in the text, it's because Mr. Spiering forgot to teach them that part.

Made in the USA
Coppell, TX
09 September 2021

62049885R00024